Two Minus One Equals One

Geoff Treasure

Two Minus One Equals One

Onwards and Upwards Publications, Berkeley House,
11 Nightingale Crescent, West Horsley, Surrey KT24 6PD

www.onwardsandupwards.org

ISBN: 978-1-907509-46-9

Cover design: Leah-Maarit

Printed in the UK

Dedication

To the memory of Lis: wife, mother and grandmother.

A lady of inexhaustible love, indomitable spirit
and unwavering faith.

Two Minus One Equals One

Contents

"Till death us do part" 7

The Unwanted Visitor 10

Why Lazarus? Why me? 12

Where was God? 30

What now? 47

What then? 67

Appendix: The Story of Lazarus 75

Two Minus One Equals One

"Till death us do part"

It was a bleak and wet February morning. The constant drizzling rain seemed determined to accompany us throughout the day. The forecast for the following days offered little encouragement of any improvement in the weather. But who cared? Certainly Lis and I were impervious to the weather as we stood at the front of a small chapel in a suburb of Bristol. The elements could do their worst. Our eyes were not on the weather but on each other. We were getting married. A new chapter in our lives was about to be written. Nothing could diminish our spirits or dampen our love for each other.

> *I, Geoff Treasure, take you, Elisabeth Thomas,*
> *To be my wife, to have and to hold*
> *From this day forward;*
> *For better, for worse,*
> *For richer, for poorer,*
> *In sickness and in health,*
> *To love and to cherish*
> *Till death us do part...*

Our sincerity as we repeated those words was of course greater than our understanding at that moment of what they would involve.

Forty three years and one month later I stood once more at the front of another church. This time I stood alone as I paid tribute to the one I had loved and cherished but from whom death had now parted me.

Our marriage had been a good one. The excitement of those early years as we established a home had been followed by the joy of family life with three lovely children who in turn presented us with seven equally loving and lovable grandchildren. As our working lives had come to an end, we had looked forward to retirement with modest hopes and dreams of what we would like to do together during those years, however many or few they might be.

On the morning of the day of Lis's retirement, however, we found ourselves in a small consulting room at the local hospital. It was to prove to be the first of many visits over the next three years.

The consultant looked at Lis.

"I am afraid that you have myeloma," he said. "It is an incurable but treatable disease."

For the next three years we were to live under a death sentence. The length of time remaining for us as husband and wife was unknown. The actual quality of that time would be revealed only as the days and the weeks went by. Our lives were to become dominated by hospital visits and treatment. Our hopes were to rise one moment, only to be dashed the next. We would have times of laughter and times of tears. There would be occasions when we would feel amongst the most blessed people in the world as we considered the way in which God had blessed us during our married life together. Equally there were moments when we would sit in silence with unanswered and unanswerable questions flashing through our minds.

We were forced to sit helplessly as a woman whose life had been characterised by vigour, joy, love and commitment to those around her was gradually weakened and finally destroyed by this monster of a disease. While we were enduring such sadness, however, we realised that we were not alone. On the one hand, countless other husbands, wives and children around the country were living through their loss. On the other hand, we realised that with us at every stage was a God whose ways were unfathomable, whose presence was constant and whose faithfulness was utterly trustworthy.

The Unwanted Visitor

John 11:12

"Lazarus is dead."

Death had come to Bethany. As it left, it took with it a man called Lazarus. Two sisters were deprived of the joy of the presence, the companionship and the support of their brother. A community lost a man who was known and loved by many. And, as so often happens, death's departure left behind misunderstanding, frustration, unanswered questions, disappointments, unrealised desires, doubts and a multitude of other emotions in the turbulent minds of those remaining.

Death has its own diary. Sometimes it sends its visitor's card in advance; at other times it turns up unexpectedly and unannounced. It may come after a prolonged illness, or it may strike with a numbing suddenness. Death may claim the life of a foetus in the womb; a child taking its first tentative and exploratory steps in a new world; a young person about to discover his or her real self, embarking upon a promising career; someone in the middle years of their life; or a person, to use a scriptural phrase, 'full of years'. His visits often seem random, meaningless and, in the minds of many, unjust. Invariably, however, those left behind find themselves grappling with a miscellany of emotions and thoughts which have to be worked through. Each death and bereavement is unique. Each person's grief and the manner in which they work through it will be individual to them. Many will have walked similar paths, but nobody will have walked *their* particular path. We cannot prescribe the course, the nature or the timing of the grieving process for anybody. To attempt to do so is to display a measure of ignorance and insensitivity which at times can only add to the burden of the bereaved. But across the diversity of individuals' grieving processes, certain common denominators can be found.

Some of these are brought before us in the story of the death of Lazarus, written for us by the Apostle John, and will offer us a basis for what follows.[1]

---

[1] See book appendix for the story as it is recounted in the Bible.

Why Lazarus? Why me?

Death's legacy to those who have loved and lost includes a bundle of unanswerable questions. A number of those questions are raised, directly or indirectly, in this passage from St John. The first question, though not stated in scripture, must have been in the minds of the immediate family and the wider circle of friends of Lazarus who later came to mourn alongside his sisters, Martha and Mary. It is a question common to all who have lost someone who was dear to them. It may be whispered in bewilderment, shouted in anger, screamed in bitterness or sobbed in deep sorrow: "Why me?" Or, in the context of the story, "Why Lazarus?"

Our knowledge of Lazarus is limited within the gospels to this and the following chapter in John. Even these scant references paint a picture of a good and much-loved man within the village community and beyond.

1. *Lazarus was a good man with qualities that not only drew others to him but even Jesus himself.*

   When his sisters wished to alert Jesus to Lazarus' physical condition, they described their brother simply as "the one you love". Jesus' own description of Lazarus as "our friend" (v.11) suggests that he considered Lazarus to be a valued and beloved friend not just of himself but of the disciples too.

2. *Lazarus, by the quality of his life, spread an influence beyond the family home and into the local communities.*

    When news of his death spread, "many of the Jews" (v.45) came to the house to comfort Martha and Mary, his sisters. The description suggests that these were not 'professional mourners' but friends and associates who wished to express in a practical manner the acute sense of loss which they had experienced by the death of Lazarus.

3. *Together with his sisters, Lazarus appears to have been a hospitable man.*

    The friendship which existed between Jesus, his disciples and Lazarus suggests previous meetings in their home at Bethany. There is little doubt, I am sure, that the hospitality shown to Jesus on these occasions was extended to many in the village who experienced warmth and hospitality at the hands of the family there. There is little doubt, therefore, that...

4. *Lazarus was regarded as a good man and loved by many.*

    And yet Lazarus had died. It would have been strange if his death had not caused a number of heads to nod in bewilderment and lips to frame the question, "But why Lazarus? He was a good man, a godly man, one who by his lifestyle endeared himself to so many people. Why has God allowed such a man to die? And the man of the house as well. It doesn't seem right at all." With their innate sense of fair play and justice, it must have appeared to many that the wrong person in Bethany had died. There were others in the village who would have been missed much less than Lazarus. There were those whose lifestyles were less attractive and endearing. Some might even suggest that others deserved to die before Lazarus. But it was Lazarus whose death they were mourning and questioning. "Why Lazarus?"

It is a short step away from a question often asked at a time of bereavement by both the sufferer prior to death and the loved ones who have experienced the loss because of the death. Why was it my wife, husband or child who died? Why do I have to experience this tragic loss? *Why me?*

Certainly both my late wife and I asked the question. For some months Lis had been in constant and acute pain in her hip and suffered from severe tiredness. Repeated visits to her local GP brought neither diagnosis nor relief. We sought checks on her blood, her thyroid, her hip. Eventually Lis requested an X-ray on her hip. Six weeks later, after further and insistent requests, her wish was granted. The results were not encouraging. Our GP prevaricated at first, suggesting that further tests were necessary before a definite diagnosis could be given. When these results became available, he tried to assure her that they could be interpreted in a number of ways. An appointment was made to meet a consultant in the Palliative Care Department of our local hospital. In a compassionate but direct way, he looked Lis in the eyes and said, "I am afraid it is myeloma. It is a cancer of the bone marrow. It is incurable but treatable."

Our reaction was no different from that of countless others who find themselves confronted with a death sentence. We cried as we drove the car from the hospital to our home, asking ourselves, "Why Lis?" The medical profession have been unable to identify a definitive cause for this particular cancer, and I suppose that while we wanted a medical answer to our question, in truth we wanted more. "Why Lis? Why not A or B or C or Z? Why Lis?"

What can we say? The chances are that if you are grieving the loss of someone close to you, that same question is often in your mind even if it is not on your lips.

Why me?

It is a natural question to ask at such times. We live in an information age. We are led to believe that all questions have answers. Type in the most obscure question on your computer, and Google will bring up a range of answers. I recall one of my teachers telling the class that the time would come when you would be able to ask people any question you like. The person addressed might be able to give you an immediate answer. More likely, however, he or she might respond, "I don't know the answer off the top of my head, but I know where I can find the answer which you seek." That was some fifty years ago and his prediction has been shown to be true in most cases. There are some questions which remain without answers, but the spirit of the age encourages us to ask the question and to expect an answer. It is natural for us to ask, "Why?" and, "Why me?"

Again, knowledge often brings control. I can still recall the time when I sat behind the driving wheel of a car for the first time. My cousin, from whom I had bought the rather battered and bruised Ford Prefect, sat alongside me and explained the rudiments of driving. Then (in retrospect quite foolishly and with a misplaced conviction of his ability to teach and my ability to learn) he encouraged me to release the brake and set off on my first drive down this desolate road. It was an unforgettable experience but for all the wrong reasons. The car swerved from one side of the road to the other, one moment increasing speed, the next almost coming to a stop. I quickly realised I did not know what I was doing. I wasn't in control of the car; the car was in control of me, and it was all rather frightening.

We like to be in control, not only of the television set or the car but of our lives as well. When sickness or death comes into our lives it creates awareness that in actual fact we are not in control. Ill health and death are uninvited intruders into our lives. They received no invitation cards. They have come at the most inconvenient times, frustrating our plans, vanquishing our hopes and bringing into our lives conditions and events over which we have no control. Suddenly we are made to realise that we cannot ultimately control our health, and we are certainly not masters of our own 'destiny'. We are subjects; we are not rulers. And the awareness of this can cause us to panic and to fear.

But such a question when addressed to God raises further issues:

1. *Is it the right question to ask at such a time as this?*

Sarah and Simon (not their real names) are two of our closest friends. They have always been a year or two ahead of us in the family stakes. They married before us, had children before us and bounced a grandchild on their knees before us. Their joy at the birth of their first grandchild, however, was tinged with some sadness when they learned that the baby girl had suffered brain damage and would require special help throughout her life. She has, incidentally, developed into a delightful young lady now and is a source of great joy for all the family. It was the words of her mother, however, that really moved me when I first heard them. "It would be easy to ask, 'Why me?'" she once said. "I believe that the more important question to ask in our situation is, 'Why *not* me?' We can give her the love and the care which she needs throughout her life." How refreshing to hear such a question when the natural thing would have been to leave out the 'not' and to simply ask, "Why me? Why have we been inflicted with this situation?"

2. *What right have we to think that because we are Christians we should be cocooned from suffering in all its forms?*

Behind such a question lies the unspoken assumption that we do not deserve to experience suffering. Others perhaps do, but we are Christians who seek to live godly lives. We look around as the Psalmist did and are tempted to ask, "Why do the evil prosper while the godly so often suffer?" Such reasoning is not the prerogative of the Christian. Those with little or no faith echo similar sentiments.

Melanie Reid is a columnist for the Times newspaper. A couple of years ago she fell from a horse and broke her neck and back. After twelve months of rehabilitation, Melanie returned to her home. In her column for the Sunday Times she wrote about a friend of hers - a fit, young, strong man who was critically ill in hospital after a sudden collapse. She wanted to offer the family comfort and support but found meaningful words difficult to come by. "Give them my love and tell them I am praying for them," she thought to herself; but the next sentence reveals the heart of her problem with suffering: "Damn it, what's the point of praying when the worst things are happening to the best people – the young and the smart and the generous and the kind and the decent – and if there really were a God, none of this would be so. Good people would be protected from this." So why was she lying paralysed at this time? She considered herself to be quite a good person, a Christian without the capital 'C', who had always tried to treat others as she would wish them to treat her - and yet the accident happened. "Yet the thunderbolt came for me all the same, didn't it... Right, that's her number up. Zapow! And that was me skewered."

But what is the basis for such thinking? Certainly it is not the Bible. Jesus is clear that bad and good things are the experience of the good and the evil, the righteous and the unrighteous alike.

Matthew 5:44-46

He causes his sun to shine on evil people and good people. He sends rain on those who do right and those who don't.

Imagine that you are walking through town when you find yourself in a sudden downpour of rain. Everyone out on this day seems to have been taken by surprise. They obviously neither expected rain nor prepared for its possibility. The shower is short but severe.

"Now," says Jesus, "look around and see how many dry shirts, jumpers and blouses you can see on people exposed to the rain."

The only people who are dry are those who took shelter. To think that they were dry because they were good while those who were wet were evil is obviously ridiculous. The rain fell upon everybody. Evil people *and* good people will, Jesus implies, get a soaking. And in the same way, after a hot summer spell it won't only be the Christians who walk around sporting a sun tan. The sun will have shone on both the evil people and the good people. The implication is, I believe, that we are all - irrespective of our faith or lack of it - exposed to common experiences. Christians cannot expect to be wrapped in divinely provided defensive armour which is guaranteed to repel all sickness and disease. The most saintly Christian and the most evil criminal serving a life sentence in prison could die on the same day with the same terminal disease.

In another passage Jesus deals with the question of other calamities. Some people who were there at that time told Jesus about certain Galileans. Pilate had mixed their blood with their sacrifices. Jesus said:

Luke 13:1-5

Some people who were there at that time told Jesus about certain Galileans. Pilate had mixed their blood with their sacrifices. Jesus said, "These people from Galilee suffered greatly. Do you think they were worse sinners than all the other Galileans? I tell you, no! But unless you turn away from your sins, you will all die too. Or what about the 18 people in Siloam? They died when the tower fell on them. Do you think they were more guilty than all the others living in Jerusalem? I tell you, no! But unless you turn away from your sins, you will all die too."

Jesus refers to incidents which must have hit the headlines at the time. Both resulted in death - one at the hands of Pontius Pilate and the other as a result of the collapse of a building. If God constantly protected the righteous from such tragedies, only the guilty would have died. The inference is of course that both good and evil people lost their lives on these occasions. The godly are not immune from such tragedies. Christians, like their ungodly neighbours and colleagues in the work place can expect to suffer from natural calamities and tragedies for which man is responsible.

3. *Is God responsible for human sickness?*

Certainly there are some Christians who would suggest so. John Calvin, one of the most influential

Christian writers, lived in the sixteenth century. He himself suffered much during his lifetime. Calvin suffered from poor digestion, migraines, kidney stones, gout, lung infections and lung haemorrhages, possibly brought on by too much preaching and teaching. In his master work, 'The Institutes of the Christian Religion', he wrote:

> *The Christian, being most fully persuaded that all things come to pass by the dispensation of God, and that nothing happens fortuitously, will always direct his eye to him as the principal cause of events, at the same time paying due regard to inferior causes in their own place ... This I say is his (sc the Christian) comfort, that his heavenly father so embraces all things under his power- so governs them at will by his nod- so regulates them by his wisdom, that nothing takes place save according to his appointment; that received into his favour and entrusted to the café of his angels neither fire, nor water, nor sword, can do him harm, except so far as God, their master, is pleased to permit.*

J. I. Packer writes:

> *The doctrine of providence teaches Christians that they are never in the grip of blind forces (fortune, chance, luck, fate); all that happens to them is divinely planned and each event comes as a new summons to trust, obey and rejoice, knowing that all is for one's spiritual and eternal good. (Romans 8.28)*

Joseph's words to his brothers as he looked back upon a lifetime of seemingly unjust treatment at the hands of so many would appear to support this. As he finally makes himself known to his brothers he says, "So then it was not you who sent me here but God." God was the ultimate author of his previous suffering; his suffering was part of the sovereign plan of God.

Joni Eareckson was a young girl when a dive into shallow waters left her with a broken neck and a paralysed body. For her suffering was no theological debate but a real desire to reconcile her faith with her suffering. Her writings have been an inspiration to so many and an antidote to some teaching on healing which is prevalent today. "Let me get this straight, God... When bad things happen, who's behind them, you or the devil? Did you permit this or was this your plan for me?"

Her conclusion was that her suffering was God's permissive will, as was Job's. The devil's plan was to "shipwreck" her faith "by throwing a wheelchair in my way ... God's motive was to thwart the devil and use the wheelchair to change me and make me more like Christ through it all." She refuses to believe that her diving accident was God's fault. She questions whether it was a direct assault from the devil. The third possibility which she offers is to ask, "Was it part of living in a fallen, wicked world and not the direct assault of either the devil or God?" This, she concludes is the most likely scenario, but she remains convinced that nothing happens in the Christian's life outside his loving plans for his sons and daughters.

I personally find it hard to align myself with those who believe God is the source of suffering. How do I reconcile this with the concept of the goodness of God? Would a good God inflict Leukaemia on a young child of three years? Would Jesus, healing with a spirit of compassion, have not been working against his Father? Would Jesus have responded to the statement of the leper ("if you are willing, you can make me clean") with the words, "I am willing. Be clean." (Mark 1:40-41)? Jesus stated very clearly his will was to do the will of God and his work was to do the work of God (John 4:34). To heal the sick would therefore appear to be a reversal and frustration of God's will if indeed God is ultimately responsible for sickness and suffering.

It is equally instructive to note the emotional reaction of Jesus to sickness. In the account of Lazarus we are told that Jesus, confronted with the weeping Mary, "was deeply moved in spirit and troubled"(v.33). The word translated 'troubled' can also imply anger. Commentators are far from unanimous in explaining the reason for Jesus' emotions, though some suggest his anger was rooted in the sight of the "concrete fact of death and sin". Jesus, we are told, was "once more deeply moved" as he approached the tomb. In verse 35 we are told that "Jesus wept". The word used differs from that employed to describe the weeping of Mary and the Jews in verse 33. Jesus wept silently although tears were visible to a bystander. Mary and her friends' weeping was more audible, "like a child".

Some translations of Mark 1:41 have the word 'anger' rather than 'compassion'. C. E. B. Cranfield accepts this more difficult reading and suggests that Jesus was angry with the disfigurement caused by the disease to one of God's creatures. Frequently it was compassion which characterised and motivated Jesus when faced with sickness and disease.

The overall picture is a reminder that...

Hebrews 4:14-16

...we do not have a high priest who is unable to feel sympathy for our weaknesses, but we have one who has been tempted in every way, just as we are – yet he did not sin.

The writer then encourages us to approach Jesus "with confidence, that we may receive mercy and find grace to help us in our time of need."

I do recognise that we live in a fallen world. We have already seen that the Christian's suffering is of the same quality as that of the non-Christian. They too can experience sickness, sorrow, poverty and death. The vital difference, as we shall see later, is their attitude towards their suffering and the work of God through their suffering.

But there are other issues raised through suffering. Behind the comments of many who hear of an individual's sickness or death is the following question:

4.　*Is there a relationship between sin and sickness?*

Such a view follows from our previous two points. When someone is diagnosed with a serious illness, there are always those who will respond with words such as,

"But he or she is such a good-living person." The implication is that they cannot associate sickness with a good life - that sickness is somehow punishment for evil in the life of the individual.

Poor old Job had to listen ad nauseam to this kind of philosophy. Job, the man who at one stage of his life had almost everything ended up with next-to-nothing - a sad figure bereft of virtually all he had and loved. He stands as the supreme example of a good man who suffered. And like us, he asked the question, "Why?" (see Job 3:11,12,16,20,23). One of his friends had the answer, or at least he *believed* that he did.

Job 4:7

Consider now: who, being innocent, has ever perished?
Where were the upright ever destroyed?
As I have observed, those who plough evil
and those who sow trouble reap it.

But his friend Eliphaz is not on the ball theologically. As David Atkinson notes in his commentary on Job: [2]

When Eliphaz affirms this (you reap what you sow) he is right. When he turns the creedal statement of Psalm one upside down and so affirms, 'Because, Job, you are reaping disaster, you must have sown iniquity,' he has left faith in the living God in favour of logic.

---

[2] David Atkinson; *The Message of Job* (p44); IVP

Eliphaz's statement is theologically incorrect and fails to provide a true answer to the question of 'innocent' suffering in general and more specifically the suffering of Job - a caring, godly and upright man

The association of sickness and sin was not uncommon in New Testament times. When Jesus healed the man who had been born blind (you can read the story in John chapter 9), the disciples asked him, "Rabbi, who sinned, this man or his parents, that he was born blind?" The inference clearly is that sickness is a punishment for sin. Jesus immediately refutes such thinking.

"Neither this man nor his parents sinned," said Jesus.

Obviously he was not indicating sinless perfection on the part of both parties. Rather he wished to dissociate sin and suffering – different to the way people commonly thought at this time. We must therefore constantly discourage the person who is ill or grieving the loss of someone dear to them from believing that their suffering is a punishment from God. To fail to do so is to run the risk of adding spiritual, mental and emotional suffering to their physical illness.

We need to acknowledge, of course, that some people do find themselves suffering because they have deliberately chosen to ignore God's rules or medical knowledge. The confirmed smoker opens up himself to numerous physical dangers from his habit; the drug addict can overdose and kill herself; the drunken driver who gets behind his wheel and kills others as a result of an accident is responsible for those deaths and the suffering of those close to him. Continuing research suggests that much of our health is determined by what we eat. In future years the responsibility for many of the cancers prevalent today may be laid at the door of those responsible for the many chemicals in our daily foods. But we can trust that God does not inflict us with our illnesses as a punishment for wrongdoing in our lives.

David Watson wrote: [3]

> *The direct equation of suffering and sin is clearly inadequate and in most cases disastrous. Is it conceivable when we see Jesus healing the sick and forgiving the sinful, that God should say, 'Ah, there's David Watson. He slipped up rather badly last month so I'll afflict him with asthma for the next twenty years.' Or later, 'He's upset me again so this time I'll destroy him with cancer.' Such thoughts are not only ridiculous: they are almost blasphemous and utterly alien to a God of infinite love and mercy as we see him so clearly in Jesus Christ.*

Those of us who have asked the question, "Why?" have come to realise that it is a question with no satisfactory answer. Some of us will continue to ask the question while accepting the futility of doing so. Sometimes the question is not as much a demand for an answer as a cry of pain or dereliction within our grieving process. We come to the point where we understand that we have to live with ignorance as to why our loved one

---

[3] David Watson; *Fear No Evil* (p113). Hodder and Stoughton

died while others live. We have to learn to live with our unanswered questions while continuing to trust in a loving, sovereign and faithful God.

Because of the finiteness of our human mind - our inability to understand fully the mind of God - we have to walk by faith. Part of that walk involves what Oss Guinness describes as "suspended judgement".

"Father," we have to say, "I do not understand you but I trust you."

There have been occasions in my life where I have needed to suspend judgement. It has been necessary for me to restate my faith in the sovereignty, the goodness and the wisdom of God in situations where I was tempted to doubt all three of these divine qualities.

Faith says, "I know that your inactivity is not because of your lack of power since you are sovereign and omnipotent. I find myself in a place where I, as a father who loves his child, would never wish my son or daughter to be. I do not believe that I am here because you delight in evil for you are a good God, full of grace and loving kindness. Finally, God, I cannot see a way out at the moment, but I cannot believe that you lack the wisdom to resolve this problem for you are an all-wise God. All I can do, therefore, is to believe that your power, love and wisdom are combining in ways I can neither see nor understand - for my good and for your glory. At such times, words must give way to silence; wrestling with God must yield to the worship of God."

Romans 11:33-36

Oh the depth of the riches of the wisdom and the knowledge of God
How unsearchable his judgements,
And his paths beyond tracing out.
Who has known the mind of the Lord?
Or who has been his counsellor?
Who has ever given to God
That God should repay him?
For from him and through him and to him are all things. To him be the glory forever.'

Where was God?

John 11:21

'Lord,' Martha said to Jesus, 'if you had been here, my brother would not have died.'

Martha, one of the sisters of Lazarus, was a confused lady. When the seriousness of her brother's illness became apparent, she had sent word to Jesus, confident that he would come to the house immediately and cure her brother of his sickness. But death came to the house before Jesus. By the time he did arrive, Lazarus had been buried for four days. But Jesus did come... eventually. When news of Jesus' impending visit reached Martha, she went out to meet him. No doubt she was in a confused state of mind, disappointed by the delayed response to her message but still welcoming with a faith which had not been destroyed by his delay and the subsequent death of her brother.

She was confident that the presence of Jesus would have brought recovery; the death of her brother was due to his absence. And yet he had known of her brother's condition. That was the mystery of the situation for her. He could have intervened, but he chose not to do so. If only Jesus had been at the house in time, Lazarus would not have died.' But Jesus wasn't and Lazarus did.

One newspaper when reporting the Dunblane massacre (the killing of 16 school children) proclaimed in its headline, "Where was God today?" It is a question commonly asked by those with no Christian faith and sometimes by those who, despite their faith, struggle to make sense of their unwelcomed circumstances. Martha's own thoughts were echoed by friends and neighbours of the family.

John 11:37

Could not he who opened the eyes of the blind man have kept this man from dying?

Martha did not doubt the power of Jesus to heal; the neighbours appeared less confident. For Martha the problem was the presence (or rather the absence) of Jesus at the time of her greatest need. C. S. Lewis had a similar experience following the death of his wife, Joy. He wrote: [4]

Meanwhile, where is God? In happy times you feel welcomed with open arms if you turn to him. Go in desperation and you feel the door is slammed in your face and double bolted. Silence. House is empty. Ever inhabited? - an absent help in time of trouble.

For some it may have seemed that the death of our loved one propelled us into a crisis with no one to help us. It is as though we were driving over sparsely populated moorland when out car spluttered and stopped. Our first reaction is to take our mobile phone and seek help. We dial but 'message failed' is the only response which we get. There is no reception in the desolated area in which we find ourselves. We get out of the car and look in vain for a

---

[4] C.S.Lewis; *A Grief Observed* (p7); Faber and Faber

telephone box or a passing motorist. There is no sign of either. We are in a dilemma. We are unsure what we should do. We walk up the road for some distance and see the welcoming light of a house in the near distance. Our spirits rise. We hasten our pace, sure that this is our salvation. Eagerly we grasp the large brass knocker in our hands and knock. Not just once or twice but, it seems, continually, incessantly, an indication of our need. We stop knocking and await a response. There is none. We shout but our shouts are absorbed into the larger and more powerful silence around us. We are alone with our need, desperate for help which is not forthcoming. The house seems empty. There is no response to our cries. We are alone in our hour of need. Where is the owner of the house?

"An absent help in time of trouble." Where is God when we need him? You yourself may have asked the question whether as a patient or a carer. Perhaps your friends and neighbours who know that we are people of faith have voiced the question to each other if not directly to us. Where is God? When we were less aware of our need of him, we felt his presence. Now we really need him, we look around and ask, "Where are you God?" We may have voiced our frustrations at his apparent silence and inactivity. The prophet Habakkuk did.

Habakkuk 1:2

How long, O Lord, must I call for help, but you do not listen? Or, cry out to you ... but you do not save?

Of course, God was where he always had been - by our side - but because he was standing in relative inactivity or speaking in such a still small voice, we neither saw him move nor heard his voice. But he was there – "a very special help in time of trouble" (Psalm 46:1). Sometimes it is only in retrospect that we recognise his faithfulness and goodness to us in such times of trouble.

In the three years between diagnosis and death, Lis and I found both negative and positive answers to our question.

1.   *God was not in the miracle cure which so many of us were praying for at the time when we received the diagnosis.*

I had read numerous books on divine healing, listened in on seminars on healings, met with people who claim to have had experience of divine healing. But if I am honest with you, I have always found the subject a difficult one.

   a.   *Some people told me that God always heals.*

"Look in the New Testament," they said, "and you find that Jesus never turned away anyone in need of healing. Jesus is unchanging. He is the same yesterday, today and forever. Be assured, therefore, that the healer in Galilee is the healer in Somerset. First century or twenty first century, Jesus heals. He wants to heal Lis of this painful and wretched disease."

I listened. I wanted to believe what I heard, but I found myself unable to rubber stamp such theology. Yes, Jesus did heal those with whom he came into contact, but there were many blind, lame, paralysed and deaf people living in the areas where healings took place who were not cured. When Jesus came to the Bethesda in John chapter five, he saw "a great number of disabled people" (v.3). One man who had been an invalid for thirty-eight years was healed by Jesus. The remainder continued to suffer with their blindness, their inability to walk and their paralysis (v.3). John gives us no indication why the one was healed but the many left with their sickness and pain.

St Paul was used by God to bring healing to some whom he met during his ministry. At Iconium, "Paul and Barnabas spent considerable time there, speaking boldly for the Lord who confirmed the message of his grace by enabling them to do miraculous signs and wonders." (Acts 14:3). When his fellow missionary, Timothy, suffered with his stomach, however, Paul encouraged him to "use a little wine because of your stomach and frequent illnesses." (1 Timothy 5:23). Clearly the very mention of his illnesses suggests that God had not stepped in and healed Timothy. Paul himself suffered with an ailment which he described as a "thorn in the flesh". Scholars are divided as to the specific nature of his illness. Paul tells us that he prayed for healing on more than one occasion. God did not respond to the request. The "thorn in the flesh" remained, but God gave him the strength to live with it, to overcome it and to manifest the grace of God through it. (2 Corinthians 3:7-10).

People with whom I spoke admitted that though they had seen God heal some people, others remained ill despite their prayers and the laying on of hands. I recall the time when the pastor of the church where we worshipped informed the congregation that his wife was terminally ill with cancer of the liver. A member of the church stood up one morning and confidently asserted that God not only wanted to heal the pastor's wife of her cancer but had done so. After her death that same person stood up in the church and denied that he had said this.

I do not doubt the power of God to heal. I believe that there are times when he steps in, and a miracle of healing is experienced. I equally believe that there are times when prayer is offered and healing sought, but the person is not healed.

We prayed for divine intervention in the progress of this disease; we prayed for healing, and we believed that God was able to bring it about. Daily we received phone calls from friends across the country assuring us of their prayers for Lis. But the more we prayed, the more the disease progressed, breaking bones in her body, causing intense pain. Where was God in all this? Not in a miracle cure.

b.   *Some people told me we needed greater faith in the willingness and the power of God to heal.*

So that was the reason Lis was not being healed! We lacked the necessary faith.

"All things are possible to those who believe," they reminded me. "Jesus was unable to perform miracles in his home town of Nazareth because of a lack of faith on the part of those who lived there. Great faith brings great healing."

According to this teaching both Lis and I needed to exercise greater faith to enable the miracle of healing to take place. I have never found such teaching a source of encouragement or help in our suffering. It seems to imply that divine healing is dependent upon me rather than upon the grace of God. It is only a short step to argue that healing is a reward for good works on the part of the children of God. My salvation was grounded in the grace of God not the works of my hands. God is a God of grace, and such teaching seems at conflict with his revealed character.

It can also so easily add guilt to the pain and the sadness already being experienced by the patient and the loved ones around him or her. Already consumed with deep sadness, all concerned are now being led to believe that death is to follow because of their lack of faith. Ultimately this teaching leaves them at the deathbed of their loved ones with the feeling that they are responsible for the death and the deprivation of divine healing. Clearly this is not so.

c. *Some told me that God had already healed Lis.*

To be honest, I did not believe the words I was hearing. (Oh, dear; what would the proponents of the teaching in the previous section think?) Only Lis and I were aware of the continuing deterioration in her health. We had received all the latest treatment available, but still the regular blood tests revealed the deterioration of her health. One person returned from a church he was visiting with the news that the preacher declared that he himself had been healed of myeloma. Wasn't this confirmation that his original pronouncement was true? God had performed the miracle we all wanted! The words were given to me as encouragement, I am sure.

But again his confidence was met with my scepticism. I wanted more answers before I was willing to believe the preacher. What type of myeloma did he have? Was he really cured or merely in remission? What was the evidence for his healing? What were his blood counts, the state of his bone marrow? On whose authority had he been declared totally healed of the disease rather than being in remission?

As these preceding paragraphs show, I have a self-confessed and on-going problem with the whole question of divine healing. I do not doubt that God has the ability to heal. I do not, however, believe that healing is available upon demand. As one person answered when asked if he believed in divine healing, "I believe that some are healed by God; others are not."

"Lord," I remember praying one night, "Lord, I believe. Help my unbelief." And I am more than ready to admit to being challenged when I read that some see because they believe while others do not believe because they do not see. For us God was not in the miracle cure. But that should not discourage you from praying for a miracle.

So where was God?

2.   God was there in the peace and the strength which he gave us.

A terminal diagnosis is not simply life-threatening but also life-changing. Time is still BC and AD but the letters have an added meaning. BC are your lives before cancer and AD are your lives after diagnosis. The past is known to you; the future is unknown. As you sit in the waiting room at the hospital for the first time, you feel that you are in another world. You wonder if you see yourself reflected in the bodies and faces of other patients alongside you. Your eyes roam the walls where notices for support groups, wigs and head coverings hang. Personal plans for the future are put on hold. You suddenly realise that your diary is going to be dictated by hospital visits and that your lives are no longer 'your own'.

I have already shared our journey home after the initial diagnosis. That evening we sat embracing each other in a state of denial and incipient anger at the prognosis. Sleep did not come easily when eventually we retired to bed. There were more tears and more embraces. I awoke in the early hours of the morning with two verses from the Bible printed indelibly upon my mind. I printed them out and placed them near our bedside where they remained until Lis passed away. One verse came from the prophet Isaiah.

Isaiah 26:2-4
You will keep in perfect peace him whose mind is steadfast, because he trusts in you.

Peace, as used in scripture, has the root meaning of 'harmony'. When a child stands by a piano and hits the notes just as he fancies, the result is discord. When an accomplished pianist sits at the piano and plays, the result is harmony. Harmony and discord is the difference between Eric Morecombe playing his version of Grieg's piano concerto ("all the right notes but not necessarily in the right order") and Andre Previn displaying his masterly skills at the keyboard. It is the difference between the surface of the sea in a storm, whipped up by the winds, and the calmness on the sea bed, unmoved by the turbulence above. It is the difference between Martha and her sister Mary, one distracted by the demands around her, rushing in all directions, mentally and emotionally distraught, and her sister sitting at the feet of Jesus. It is the difference between the disciples on the Sea of Galilee, fearing for their lives, wondering if Jesus cared about them and Jesus himself, asleep in the stern of the boat. It is that gift of God which enabled Peter to sleep soundly the night before his possible execution; Paul and Silas to sing hymns of praise in the Philippian prison and to assure the Philippian church, as the apostle awaited the result of his appeal, that for him to live was Christ and to die was gain.

The prognosis of a terminal illness is a new experience for many of us. It catapults you into the unknown with the potential to strip you of your confidence as your mind confronts you with a myriad of questions for which you have no definite answer. How long? What if? When? How will death come? What will the pathway to death be like? Will I be able to be strong enough? And as a carer, will I be able to provide the love and the care my wife needs and deserves? Will I be strong enough as I watch her suffer, knowing that although I can bring comfort, I cannot stem the march of the disease?

I recall saying to Lis just after the diagnosis, "I do hope that I can be a good enough husband for you in the future."

"Of course you will," she replied in her usual loving way.

But for me the questions were real and the answers at the time, unknown.

We had our difficult times. We awaited the results of ongoing tests with apprehension; we wondered when and how the end would come and what demands would be made upon us in the months ahead. But throughout, both Lis and I enjoyed that peace which really does pass all human understanding. As long as we were able to keep our eyes upon God instead of the circumstances in which we found ourselves, we experienced his peace. The peace of God enabled us to face the certainty of death, the prospect of separation, the unknowns before us, the highs and the lows of treatment, the failure of medication to sustain progress, the presence of death hovering around us, the eventual presence of death, the multitude of administrative demands upon the death of a loved one, the belief that life continues with a divine purpose for the one who is left.

The second verse given to me that night came from 2 Corinthians.

2 Corinthians 12:9

But he said to me, "My grace is all you need. My power is strongest when you are weak." So I am very happy to brag about how weak I am. Then Christ's power can rest on me.

"But surely," I thought that morning, "this verse has the power to answer all my questions, to disperse my fears and to dispel my anxieties, if I can accept it by faith as a word from God to us both at this time of our lives."

Paul, you will recall, had been suffering from an unknown disease, his "thorn in the flesh". He had pleaded with God to remove it and to bring him wholeness. God had assured him that while the thorn would remain in his flesh and God would not provide healing, nevertheless God would provide him with strength in his weakness and his grace in his sense of personal insufficiency to meet the demands of the hour. And now God had given us that promise.

He was promising that he would be our sufficiency. He was assuring us that at times when we felt weak, unable to stand, when we felt that we lacked the resolve and the power to fight, he would infuse us with his divine power. His power would be our strength. As we were drained of our natural strength, his divine power would flow in to fill the void. And his grace? That would be sufficient for our every need. I came to love that word 'sufficient'.

Many years ago I bought an old, second hand leather case. It was a special one with expanding hinges. If there was very little placed in the case, the hinges would adjust to the size of the contents and close neatly. The greater the contents placed in the case, the more the hinges would expand, and the case would enfold the clothes placed within it. There was always expansion according to the burden within the case. God's grace, we were assured, would be like that: sufficient in week one, in year two and towards the end of year three of my wife's illness. Sufficient for Lis. Sufficient for me. Divine power for the hour and grace for the moment. These were our needs and God's provision.

Strength was needed in different areas of our lives. Lis needed physical strength to do those things which she wanted to do. Tiredness is one of the symptoms of myeloma, and relatively small exertion brought a sense of physical weakness. The disease brought immense pain at times. Ribs and clavicle bones were destroyed by the myeloma, causing intense pain which medication did not always control. There was the need for emotional empowerment. How do you manage when you know that your life is coming to an end, bringing separation from the ones you love - spouse, children, grandchildren - who had brought so much joy into your life? Towards the end of her life, Lis found it difficult to read the thoughts I had been accustomed to expressing in cards or to accept verbal expressions of my love for her. At that stage human love and relationships were temporary. Love expressed on a human level had a 'best before' date, so to speak, and every expression of love was an audible and emotional reminder of that fact. Spiritual strength was needed. Spiritual battles were being waged. Mental strength was weakened at times by the sheer amount of chemicals in her body. But throughout we discovered that the grace of God was sufficient and that his power was a source of strength when human strength was ebbing. God was faithful.

3.   *God was there in the providential care he showed us.*

For a number of years Lis and I had lived in London where I had been the head teacher of a Church of England comprehensive school. Upon taking early retirement I was offered the post of Consultant in the South West for a large Anglican para-church organisation. We discussed the possibility of a move and were in agreement that we would return to the West Country. It was a difficult and a costly move. For months Lis was extremely unhappy, and I in turn felt guilty for moving her from friends and job satisfaction to a new area of the country. Those early months were very difficult for us both. She eventually found a most fulfilling job where she was extremely happy and embraced a large circle of loyal and faithful friends. What neither of us knew at the time of our move was the future diagnosis or the provision for treatment in the town in which we were to live. In his providential care, God had brought us to an area where Lis would be able to receive the most wonderful treatment during the three years of her illness.

Myeloma is one of the rarer forms of cancer. On average a local GP may come across one case in his career. Little is known about the cause of the disease and a cure has yet to be found for it. Imagine our surprise then, when we discovered that our local hospital was a recognised treatment centre for that specific form of cancer. We were in the right place at the right time.

There we found a wonderful consultant who was recognised widely for his work on myeloma. Over the three years Lis was treated we both grew to respect, admire and love the man. Whenever we were with him we felt that Lis was the only patient for whom he was responsible, such was the care he showed. She was never 'Mrs Treasure' but always 'Lis'. Lis always felt more confident when she left his consulting room. He had the power to encourage and to raise the spirits. He made himself constantly available for us. If we had a concern, we were free to phone him at any hour of the day. If he was unavailable at that precise moment, you could be assured that he would return the telephone call when he was free to do so. When Lis died, he sent me a card with personal sentiments about Lis. We had the right man in the right place at the right time.

Because of the importance of the hospital for the study of myeloma, we discovered that we had access to all the latest treatments, including those not normally prescribed by NICE, the official body which monitors effectiveness and cost of new drugs. Lis was also granted a bone marrow transplant which sadly proved effective for a very short time only. Regretfully, none of the treatment brought long term results; but no treatment was withheld, in the hope of prolonging her life. All that could have been done was done. We were in the right place at the right time with the right provision and the right personnel. And God, in his providential care, had planned it for us years before the disease was diagnosed.

4. *God was there in the death Lis died.*

It was Woody Allen who said that while he was not afraid of death, he didn't want to be there when it happened. And that is probably true for most of us. As Christians we do not fear death itself; many may fear the manner of dying. My wife did. I recall a conversation with her one evening in which she expressed these 'fears'. I tried to assure her that when the time of death came, she would probably be in a deep sleep and unaware of slipping into the presence of God. I was fearful too. I had heard stories of some painful deaths, and I wondered how I would react if such a death was hers. But God was so good to us in her passing.

God gave us a dress rehearsal. Just before Christmas, the year prior to her death, Lis's condition deteriorated and she was hospitalised. She was in much pain and a confused state of mind. The consultant came to visit her in the ward and told us that she probably had anything from between two hours and two days to live. To us it looked like hours. The family were gathered around her bed in the side ward where she was sleeping. We took it in turns to hold her hand. We prayed, we watched and we analysed her every breath. It was hard to believe, but to be in the presence of death was like being in heaven. Those hours were most precious to us all. There was a peace and a divine presence in that room which comforted and strengthened us all. We all felt that the end of her life was imminent.

Lis, however, had other ideas. About four o'clock in the morning she sat up, drank three cups of tea, ate some cherries and began talking about coming home. Sadly there was to be a short period in the local hospice before she came home two days before Christmas. That same night Lis joined me at the local Christingle service. As she had stubbornly told the staff at the hospice, she had to prepare a Christmas meal for fourteen, and sure enough, on Christmas day, she did just that!

The following March she died. But that experience in the hospital ward took away all fear from us and prepared us for her eventual passing.

When she died, to our understanding she knew nothing. (That in itself was an answer to our prayers.) The evening before her death she intimated to her sister that she could no longer fight. It seemed here she was giving herself permission to die. On the morning of the day of her death, before lapsing into unconsciousness, she had phoned a friend to arrange to meet up later in the week. The children were able to travel down to be with her as she took three deep breaths and passed into the presence of God. It was the end of a beautiful life for us and the beginning of an even more wonderful one for her. "Precious in the sight of God is the death of his saints," said the Psalmist. And it was precious to us also. She lay there at rest and peace, free from the marks of the pain which had characterised the previous three years of her life. Loss and gain, sadness and joy, sorrow and deep gratitude all mingled together in our hearts. God had been so good to us all.

What now?

John 11:44

Take off the grave clothes and let him go.

For the family of Lazarus there was great joy because there was resurrection and reunion. Jesus had shown himself to be the resurrection and the life by bringing back to life the brother and friend whom Jesus, Martha and Mary had lost. The day would come when death would visit that household again, but for the present death had been defeated by life.

For those of us who have loved and lost there is great sadness and sorrow. A loving relationship has been terminated through no fault of ourselves. Two have become one. 'We' is now 'me'. Companionship has been replaced by aloneness. Plans and hopes have been dashed. An unknown future lies ahead with all of its demands on the one hand and our human frailty on the other. To the question, "What now?" is added the second, "*How* now?" New responsibilities, fresh pressures, previously inexperienced experiences will certainly confront us. Two minus one equals one, and it is all new to us. *What now?*

After the loss comes the grief. There was a sense in which I had been grieving for three years since the day the terminal diagnosis was given to us. But death brings a grief which is more real and raw. It was a new path for me. I had much to learn. I had to learn to...

1. Be patient.

> *a. There is no 'one size fits all' hat for those who are grieving.*

Pick up the text books on bereavement and you will be told that we all go through a grieving process. We will all at some time be in a state of...

- **Denial**

  "I can't believe that this has happened. I wait for him to come through the door for his tea."

- **Anger**

  ...at the GP, the medical staff, even yourself and, for some, anger directed towards God.

- **Guilt**

  "My wife was younger than me; I should have gone first." "Could I have done more? Did any of my decisions in our lives cause the illness? Did I care enough during the last months?"

- **Low spirits**

  "I don't want to go out. I don't want to meet with friends. Social occasions are not for me. I feel worse rather than better in my spirit after them." For some depression sets in; for others there are physical symptoms.

What we must constantly remember is the uniqueness of our situation. You are you. Your spouse was your spouse, with a relationship which nobody else enjoyed with him/her. Your experiences of the death of your loved one was a personal journey which no other person has experienced. It follows, therefore, that your grief will be personal and unique to you. Nobody else can or should attempt to prescribe the pattern or the length of your grieving process. When people say, "He/she should be over it by now," ignore them. Their sentiments are evidence of their inability to understand the personal nature of the grieving process. Grieve in the way you need to, at the speed you need to, remembering that you are you!

b.   Grief is unpredictable.

You think it is gone, and suddenly it is there again! I recall sitting outside of a hotel in Corfu with Lis and reading extracts from the memoirs of Tony Benn. In this excerpt he was recalling the death of his wife and was observing the unpredictability of expressions of grief. He wrote: [5]

> *I was listening to the cassettes in the car, and I began crying, and I sobbed and sobbed all the way to Stansgate ... it just comes back to you all of a sudden.*

And that is the unpredictability of grief. A thought, a place, a dialogue on the television, a glance at a photograph can all be enough to cause the tears to flow. If you are in company you may embarrassed. If you are alone you may feel pleased that the loss is still as real as the first

---

[5] Tony Benn; *More Time for Politics; Diaries 2001-2007*; Hutchinsons

day, though surprised that the process which you once thought was over is obviously not.

There will be times in the immediate years following the death of your loved one when you almost dare to believe that your grieving has ended. The next day you can find yourself in the pit of despair and self-pity, angry with yourself for being in a place which you thought you had left. That is the unpredictability of grief. It does not take a quick walk along a straight, unbending road out of your life. Rather the road is a spiral along which grief returns and comes back to encircle you.

    c.   You are undertaking a major rebuilding project. And that takes time.

Rome, says the old proverb, wasn't built in a day. Shattered lives are not rebuilt in a day, and the death of a loved one shatters one's life. You may have dropped a china vase and, to your dismay, have seen the pieces scattered across the kitchen floor. Your first reaction, perhaps, is anger and self-blame. You then pick up the pieces and assess the situation. Should it be binned or can it be reassembled? You decide upon the latter. Of course it will never be quite the same as it originally was, but it will have a future. The repair will take time, skill and patience, but it can be done.

When you lose your spouse, you may have lost a husband/wife, a friend, a lover, an adviser, a spiritual guide, a counsellor, a companion, a financial adviser, a gardener, a home decorator, a help mate, a holiday companion - the list is personal and endless. Each role that your spouse played creates a gap. The gap may become a source of anxiety: "But she looked after all the finances. Where do I begin?"; "How can I possibly keep the garden under control?"; "No more holidays for me."; "I'm no DIY expert, and I can't afford professional prices. What am I going to do?"

We must realise that not everything needs to be done at once. We need to prioritise - first things first. And then, if we continue to feel utterly helpless, search out a family friend or a support group where help may become available. But throughout, remember, it is a long term project upon which you have embarked.

d. Be patient with friends and family.

Don't have great expectations of other people. You may be preparing for disappointment. That may seem a strange thing to say. Many of them were so good to you at the time of the death of your loved one. A few of them invited you to their home for a meal, and others promised to invite you for coffee. And possibly they did for the first few months. You appreciated their love and care for you. But past experience is no guarantee of future expressions of compassion and care.

There will be one or two faithful friends who will continue to do so, but the majority will fall away. After six months they may feel that you have adapted to your new situation, are making your own way in the world and no longer need their support. It is more likely that they have such busy lives of their own that you are only in their thoughts when face to face with them. That is when the promises are made. The subsequent days rarely see the fulfilment of those promises. Those who do not expect anything will not be disappointed. Those who do expect are sometimes disappointed.

"I must put on a brave face," say some who are grieving. The braver the face you show to those around, the more they believe that you are overcoming your loss, and the greater the strength they perceive you to have. That combination may lead to them believing that their meals and coffee are superfluous. Only you know that they are not.

In extreme cases, the bereaved may find that some folk will cross to the other side of the road in order to avoid a conversation with them. C. S. Lewis felt this avoidance so acutely that he wrote: [6]

> *I am aware of being an embarrassment to everyone I meet ... Perhaps the bereaved ought to be isolated in special settlements like lepers.*

e.   Prepare for limited conversations.

Even when you are in other people's company conversation may be difficult for them. In a way, you are the issue - the reason for long silences, less confident comments or what you may consider to be inane observations. People are unsure what to say. They are not sure how you are feeling at that moment, only that you have lost someone very dear to you. The wrong word may

---

[6] C.S.Lewis; *A Grief Observed* (p4); Faber and Faber

have the opposite effect to that intended by your friend. The last thing they want to do is to reduce you to tears, which will wash away any small confidence they might have had at the beginning of the conversation. After the initial greeting they may need to say nothing at all. In some cases their very presence may be a comfort to you. Equally you may simply value a listening ear. When you spend long hours alone in the house, the opportunity to talk to someone may be grasped with alacrity.

- **People are reminded of their own mortality.**
  C. S. Lewis described himself as "death's head". He felt that whenever he stood before another person or couple he was, in fact, a vivid reminder that his experience would be theirs at some time in the unknown future - a fact they would rather not face. Death is the one common denominator in everybody's life. "We sometimes think what would happen if one of us dies," they say. Reality doesn't have an 'if' in its vocabulary but only a 'when'. That unpleasant truth stated by your presence can make conversation difficult.

- **People are reluctant to talk about your loved one.**
  For me it was one of the saddest aspects of those early months of grieving. It was as though by her death my wife had been eradicated from others' memories. She was my constant companion, my lover, the object of my affection, my friend, my mother, my counsellor, my

teacher, my curate, my deputy head and so much more. Of course I wanted to talk about her, and I was saddened when those around neither took the initiative to do so or ignored the opportunities which I offered them in my conversations. There were times when I almost wanted to make a badge to wear announcing to those around, "I am happy to talk about Lis." Not everyone feels the same as I did, of course. Joyce Oates, in her book, 'A Widow's Story'[7] admits that she became resentful of people's enquiries. She even admits that at one point she toyed with the idea of having a T-shirt printed with the words, "Yes my husband died. Yes, I am very sad. Yes, you are kind to offer condolences. Now can we change the subject?" One of the loveliest things said to me was spoken by a couple whom I had recently got to know within the church. We had much in common and soon struck up a good relationship. "Tell me all about Lis," said the wife, "so that we can understand you better." What compassion on their part and what joy on mine as I introduced them to a little of the Lis they had never known.

---

[7] Published by Fourth Estate

- **People are not on the same wavelength as you with their language.**

  Be prepared for well-worn clichés. A cliché is an expression that has become stale from too much use. When a cliché was first used it was of great comfort and meaning. It was so good that those who heard it made a mental note and thought, "I'll use that when it's suitable to do so." But constant repetition has devalued the original value of the saying. Clichés still slip off the tongue in a given situation, and you may find yourself bombarded with them. In your quieter moments you may re-evaluate them and often conclude that they are almost meaningless and worthless. That is not to undervalue the sincerity with which they were addressed to the bereaved.

  "How are you?"

  It's a natural enough opener for a conversation. We use it every day. It is a question you will find is the opening gambit for most conversations. I used to ask myself, "Do they *really* want to know how I am feeling at this moment? If I unburdened myself to them, would they ever ask me that question again?"

  "She is in a better place."

  There are occasions in conversation when your head says one thing but your heart feels another. Your head acknowledges that Lis is with Christ which, as Paul says, "is far better". But in the lonely winter evening or the prolonged weekends, you may be forgiven for thinking, "A better place? What better place is there than sitting beside me, walking along hand in hand, talking, and laughing together?"

"God is good."

Again your head says, "Yes, God is good, and he has been good to us throughout our lifetime." But the concept of the goodness of God and the presence of suffering and evil in the world is one of the great stumbling blocks to faith for many people. Our finite understanding of the true love of God when viewed against the months of pain (which we had to witness with an acute sense of helplessness) perhaps led us, when at our lowest, to question the goodness of God. "God is good," exclaims the minister. "All of the time," responds the congregation. And if God is good all of the time (as He is) we have to accept that truth in faith, sometimes against all the evidence.

"God wanted her to be with him."

I remember someone saying that to me in a house group. I smiled outwardly, but inwardly I was thinking, "And I wanted her with me too. If, as Peter assures us, a thousand years is like a day with God, couldn't he have waited a little longer?"

f.   *Prepare for broken promises.*

People around you are kind and often make promises in the utmost sincerity: "You must come around for tea."; "We must have a day away on the coast."; "You must come and have a meal with us." You thank them and wait. So often the promises are unfulfilled, and you feel a sense of disappointment. You ask yourself how much you really mean to them - was the promise simply a throwaway line?

g. *Prepare for judgements.*

The months following bereavement can be times of confusion, indecision and, sometimes, of wrong decisions. You are in a position, not of your choice, where you have to reassess the rest of your life. 'Me' has replaced 'we'. You wonder what the future holds for you, who will care for you if you are unwell. You try to fill your days with busyness but your heart is often not in the activity as you realise you are only seeking to fill your days. Some people make decisions which surprise and sometimes upset those dearest to them. Be true to yourself. Unless others have sat where you are sitting, they should be less hasty in their judgements.

"She should be getting over his death by now."

"He still seems so bitter and resentful."

"He is seeing someone already. His wife's body can't be cold yet in the grave."

"She keeps his bedroom like a shrine. Time she got rid of his belongings."

"What, re-married already?"

It is hard not to get upset by such comments. Remember that your feet are in your shoes. Nobody else is walking in them along your path.

Patience is never easy. "Lord, give me patience, but make it quick" is a prayer we all entertain at times. The operation is over and the surgeon stands at the foot of the bed.

"When will I be able to go home?" is often the first question the patient asks.

A smile and a nod greet the question. "You are not really aware of the immensity and gravity of the treatment which you have received," replies the surgeon. "We have got to get you better first, and that is going to take time."

That which is true of the physical body is equally true of grief.

2. *Be positive.*

It's hard to be positive when your whole world feels negative. It is difficult to feel encouraged when there is so much around to discourage you. But there is a world of difference between the 'en' and the 'dis' in these two related words. To feel encouraged puts more courage into your spirit. To be discouraged is to drain you of your existing courage. When life is hard you need more rather than less courage to face each day. So while the very thought of being positive at the beginning of your bereavement may seem a hard call, such positivity can help you along the way.

    a. *Think of the blessings which are yours even in your difficult situation.*

The old hymn I used to sing as a child suddenly had new meaning for me.

Count your blessings,
Name them one by one;
Count your blessings,
See what God has done;
Count your blessings,
Name them one by one;
And it will surprise you what the Lord has done. [8]

I remember our first visit for radiotherapy. We sat in the waiting room and looked around us. We saw children in arms with scars across their young heads which we assumed indicated surgery for the removal of a tumour. What life had those children seen? What was their life expectancy? We saw teenagers joking with their friends and wondered what their prognosis was. Young married couples joined us. We sat there knowing we had experienced forty plus years of a very happy marriage, the blessings of three loving and supportive children and seven grandchildren who had been a source of constant joy to us. How many of those sitting alongside us had been blessed in that way? We had a vibrant Christian faith which gave us strength and courage, comfort and convictions. What feelings, fears, disappointment and despair were those around us suffering? Where did they find strength for each new day?

We had so much for which to thank God - a long and blessed past even if the immediate future was uncertain.

---

[8] Rev. J. Oatman; *Count Your Blessings*

b.   Thank God for the memories which you will always have.

The longer you have been married, the greater may seem your sense of loss. But the longer you have been married, the greater the bank of memories which you have stored over the years. Memories are no real substitute for the person, but memories are means whereby we can hold on in a sense to the one we loved and relive some of the good times we enjoyed together.

In the early days of your grief, memories may drag you down. Memories are by their very nature things of the past, and you are living in the present with an unknown and an uncertain future. At time passes, however, your memories may become a resource for smiles and joy as you remember the happy times you had together, the places that you visited, the holidays you enjoyed, the jokes which caused you to share laughter. Some people find it difficult to return to places where they enjoyed their spouse's company. Others, me included, can sit in cafes, drive to scenic spots, return to holiday haunts and find the memories which they evoke a comfort. The individuality of grief means you alone know whether or not this is for you.

c.   Believe that God still has future plans for you.

I recall the consultant at our first meeting, asking us what plans we had for the future.

"After what you have told us," I replied, "I don't think we have any plans."

The implication was that we felt we had no future. In retrospect it wasn't a truthful answer. Of course we had a future, though its nature was uncertain and its length unknown. Lis never stopped planning for her future. She booked holidays and bought clothes. Perhaps that was a source of strength and confidence for her. In the television drama of the life of Mo Mowlem, there was a scene when she returned from shopping with a number of bags and enough clothes to restock her wardrobe. Her husband was amazed and actually said words to the effect of, "What are you buying new clothes for? You have no future." Her spirited response showed that Mo, the battler, knew that she had *some* future and that the alternative was simply to curl up in her pyjamas and await death. That, she was not prepared to do. What the dying want for themselves is no different to what they want for the ones they leave behind.

When a person suffers bereavement, it can seem for a time that life has ended. Jonathan Tropper wrote in his work of fiction (one which was obviously based upon real experiences), "I had a wife. Her name was Hailey. Now she's gone and so am I." The death of a wife or husband may appear at the time to be a death sentence for the one left bereaved. Occasionally we read of an elderly couple dying within days of each other. Did emotional death precede physical death?

Even though the husband or wife remaining lives on, they may feel that a part of them died with their spouse's death. And what are they to make with the part that remains? Has their future a purpose? On more than one occasion I felt that for the rest of my life I would be treading water. The best was past. The future might have a superabundance of time, but how was I to use it? Did God still have a plan for my life, or did that end with retirement and the death of my wife?

It took me some time to realise afresh that, yes, God still had plans for me and that when the time was right he would reveal them to me and to others around me.

> d.   *Think of ways in which you can develop yourself and your ministry to others.*

The loss of your loved one has brought about not only changes but also opportunities. Although your day is still of twenty four hours' duration, the amount of time alone has increased. How that time is used is a choice which we have to make. Spend it alone and you may find yourself growing introspective and overwhelmed with a sense of self-pity or anger; you will think only of what you used to do with your partner and sit and feel sorry for yourself with your loss. Alternatively use that time to extend your range of interests and skills. Open your home to others and offer other lonely people hospitality. Become more involved in the life of your church. Find ways in which you can become involved in voluntary work where your skills and interpersonal qualities will be enrichment to others as well as to yourself. Don't give up, but grow up.

3.   Be perceptive.

Ronald Dunn is a well-known Christian minister in the States with a number of books to his name. His life was shattered in 1978 when his son, Ronnie, took his own life. His book 'When Heaven is Silent' is an account of his personal experience following the death of his son.

Towards the end of the book Ronald Dunn has a chapter entitled, 'The most unbelievable verse in the Bible.' It is found in Paul's letter to the Romans where he writes:

Romans 8:28
And we know that in all things God works for the good of those who love him, who have been called according to his purpose.

How can you reconcile this with the suicide of your son? His first reaction was to "look for loopholes in this verse". Perhaps the translators had got it wrong. Perhaps Paul never really meant that at all. He studied a range of commentaries, compared translations before concluding: [9]

As I write I am surrounded by stacks of commentaries on the book of Romans, the latest and the greatest, and by piles of papers and notes I have searched through a hundred times and I must tell you - I have found no loophole.

It is an amazing verse which speaks with certainty ("we know") and the voice of experience that...

...in all things which we experience...

...God is at work...

...for the good of those who love him and have been called according to God's purpose.

Now these words are not telling us that every experience we have is good in itself or that in a human

---

[9] Ronald Dunn; *When Heaven is Silent* (p186); Word Books

sense everything will be fine in the end. It is promising, however, that God is able to use human experiences for our good and for his glory. And that is a declaration of faith in God. To the widow or widower, mother or father standing beside an open grave and watching the coffin being lowered, Paul's words may seem to make no sense at all. But only the first page is being written at that time. The rest of the book will show to the spiritually discerning eye the veracity of Paul's statement. Paul is not alone in his confidence. Equally amazing is the word of James to his readers:

James 1:2-4

Consider it pure joy, my brothers, whenever you face trials of many kinds, because you know that the testing of your faith develops perseverance. Perseverance must finish its work so that you may be mature and complete, not lacking anything.

"Consider testing and trials as pure joy? What planet is this man on?" you might be tempted to ask. But that is what James is encouraging his readers to do. The reason is that the unwanted and at times unwelcomed experiences which crash into our lives can ultimately become constructive rather than destructive forces. With God's help they will enrich rather than impoverish, construct rather than destruct, develop me as a Christian rather than impede my development. It is not what testing and hardship can do to us but what God can do for us with that testing.

In the months and years following bereavement it is good to take stock and try to see just what God has been doing in your life.

- How has God been making you more like Jesus? Are you more understanding than you once were? Do you display compassion to others in a way you might never have been able to do so had you not experienced bereavement? Do you commend rather than criticise those around you? Are you less selective in your friendships and reaching out to others in a way which might surprise you? Can you see things for which to be grateful, and do you share your gratitude with God? Are you less bitter? Have you become more prayerful? Have your experiences caused you to draw nearer to God rather than to push him further away? Do you enjoy a peace with God and experience the peace of God in your daily life? Do others notice the growth in your personal life?

- Have you surprised yourself by what you have achieved? Are you managing your finances and keeping on top of work in the home? Have you been able to get out of the house and enjoy the company of others in new environments? Have you developed new interests and skills? Have you made new friends? Have you been able to visit places from the past? Have you developed a desire to holiday? Are you feeling more fulfilled than you once did? Have you set yourself simple targets and reached them? Do you laugh and smile? Do others enjoy your company rather than dread it? Have you, along with Paul, learned the secret of contentment?

- Can you identify how God has been at work for your good and his glory in your life? Then thank him and praise him for what he has done.

What then?

John 11:23

Jesus said to her, 'Your brother will rise again.'

"...in sure and certain hope of the resurrection to eternal life through our Lord Jesus Christ who will transform our frail bodies that they may be conformed to his glorious body who died, was buried and rose again for us. To him be glory forever. Amen."

These words from the Anglican funeral service put a whole new perspective upon death. They speak with conviction and with clarity. Death is not the end. It is simply a door through which Christians pass and find the fulfilment of eternal life on the other side. There will be transformation as well as resurrection. The body which we laid in the ground - wracked by pain, broken through disease - will be transformed to be like the glorious resurrection body of Jesus Christ. Pain, suffering and tears will be no more for the loved one we have buried.

Pie in the sky? Wishful thinking? That is the view of many today. It was a notion held by many of the people in the city of Corinth when Paul preached the resurrection of the dead to them. "The dead," they said, "do not rise." (1 Corinthians 15:12). In response the Apostle wrote that glorious and definitive section in his letter. The theme was resurrection and it was stated as a "sure and certain hope". Hope in the New Testament is unfulfilled certainty. Not for Paul a nebulous philosophical hope. The resurrection of Christians was as sure and certain as the resurrection of Jesus Christ which was central to the gospel he preached and the basis of his transformed life and ministry. Paul himself had met with the risen Christ on the road to Damascus and lived with him every day subsequent to his conversion. He was equally sure that he would meet him again on the day of resurrection.

"To deny the resurrection of the body, full stop," he wrote to the Corinthians, "is to write off all the evidence for the resurrection of Jesus Christ." For Paul the evidence for the physical resurrection of Jesus was beyond doubt. Paul had talked with Peter who had, I am sure, recounted in detail the events of that first Easter. As an eye witness he would have described events leading up to the arrest of Jesus, the trial before the Sanhedrin, the crucifixion, his burial in the tomb of a secret disciple, Joseph, who was also a member of the Jewish Court which had condemned Jesus. And then with great excitement Peter would have recounted his own experiences at the tomb where Jesus had been buried; his amazement at the message which Mary Magdalene had brought him on the first day of the week when she announced, "They have taken the Lord out of the tomb, and we don't know where they have put him."; the problem of the empty tomb and the missing body!

Peter would have described to Paul how he left everything and ran with speed to the tomb to find the stone rolled away, the tomb empty, the shroud in which Jesus had been buried lying there on the shelf as though the body of Jesus had passed through it.

"We went back mystified. We knew the disciples had not taken the body. We couldn't understand why the enemies of Jesus would have done so. After all it was they who had asked for a military guard around the tomb to thwart any attempt to steal the body by Jesus' friends. They knew that Jesus had prophesied resurrection. They didn't believe it but were determined to avoid any scam suggesting that he had.

"And then we saw him. He came to us in a room where doors and windows were locked. He showed Thomas the scars on his body which he had suffered at his crucifixion. He later met us on the beach; he ate with us and talked with us. We knew he was alive."

For Paul there was no doubt. Jesus had died, had been buried and had risen again. It was his encounter with the risen Christ that had transformed his life, given him a mission to share the good news about Jesus with both Jew and Gentile and sustained him through a life of rejection, suffering and pain.

1 Corinthians 15:20

Christ has indeed been raised from the dead, the first fruits of those who have fallen asleep.

No resurrection from the dead? The idea was totally unacceptable to the apostle.

"If you rule out any possibility of resurrection, the consequences are immense," he argued.

"If Jesus did not rise from the dead... (v13)

➢ My preaching is of no value at all. (v14)

➢ When we preach resurrection, we are leading you all up the garden path with deceit and lies. (v15)

➢ There will be no resurrection for believers who die. (v18)

➢ Your faith in Christ is futile. (v27)

➢ You are still under judgement for your sin. (v18)

➢ We Christians, who have put our trust in Christ are deluded and deserve the pity of our peers. (v19)

And then follows the great 'but' of confidence and hope.

1 Corinthians 15:20-22

But Christ has indeed been raised from the dead, the first fruits of those who have fallen asleep. For since death came through a man, the resurrection of the dead comes also through a man. For as in Adam all die, so in Christ all will be made alive.

In those verses lie the reason why Christians who have lost those whom they loved do not "grieve like the rest of men who have no hope" (2 Thessalonians 4:13). We weep, we mourn, and we experience loneliness, sadness and sorrow in the same manner as unbelievers who are bereaved. But we have a value added tax to our grief - the sure and the certain hope of the resurrection.

Like the Corinthians we may have our questions about resurrection:

1 Corinthians 15:35

But someone may ask, 'How are the dead raised? With what kind of body will they come down?

The Christian sees evidence of life after death each spring when trees sprout their leaves, bulbs produce their flowers and new spring life comes from what appeared to be autumn death. They recognise that their creator God has created life and endowed that life with a variety of bodies - heavenly and earthly bodies, bodies for the land and the sea, for animals and for humans. The rich diversity of creation makes the resurrection body just another facet of his creative handiwork. Its exact nature is unknown at the present and waits to be revealed at the resurrection.

Of one thing Paul is certain:

1 Corinthians 15:43-44

The body that is sown is perishable, it is raised imperishable; it is sown in dishonour, it is raised in glory; it is sown in weakness, it is raised in power; it is sown a natural body, it is raised a spiritual body.

David Watson wrote:

When I die, it is my firm conviction that I shall be more alive than ever, experiencing the full reality of all that God has prepared for us in Christ. Sometimes I have foretastes of that reality, when the sense of God's presence is especially vivid. Although such moments are comparatively rare, they whet my appetite for much more. The actual moment of dying is shrouded in mystery, but as I keep my eyes upon Jesus I am not afraid. Jesus has already been through death for us and will be with us when we walk through it ourselves. In those great words of the twenty third Psalm,

Even though I walk through the valley of the shadow of death I fear no evil; for thou are with me. [10]

1 Corinthians 15:51-58

Listen, I tell you a mystery: We will not all sleep, but we will all be changed - in a flash, in the twinkling of an eye, at the last trumpet. For the trumpet will sound, the dead will be raised imperishable, and we will be changed. For the perishable must clothe itself with the imperishable, and the mortal with immortality. When the perishable has been clothed with the imperishable, and the mortal with immortality, then the saying that is written will come true: Death has been swallowed up in victory. Where, O death, is your victory? Where, O death, is your sting? The sting of death is sin, and the power of sin is the law. But thanks be to God! He gives us the victory through our Lord Jesus Christ. Therefore, my dear brothers, stand firm. Let nothing move you. Always give yourselves fully to the work of the Lord, because you know that your labour in the Lord is not in vain.

---

[10] David Watson; *Fear No Evil* (p168). Hodder and Stoughton

What a comfort to those who have lost the ones they love. What a joy for those who have watched wife, husband, parent or child waste away with a body ravaged by disease. A new, resurrection body! The blind will see, the lame will walk, the heart will be renewed, the cancerous cells replaced by healthy ones, no longer with a demented mind but a whole mind. And whether we have died before the return of Christ or are witness of that tremendous event, a reunion will take place. We shall be reunited with the risen Christ and with those whom we love.

1 Thessalonians 4:13-18

Brothers, we do not want you to be ignorant about those who fall asleep, or to grieve like the rest of men, who have no hope. We believe that Jesus died and rose again and so we believe that God will bring with Jesus those who have fallen asleep in him. According to the Lord's own word, we tell you that we who are still alive, who are left till the coming of the Lord, will certainly not precede those who have fallen asleep. For the Lord himself will come down from heaven, with a loud command, with the voice of the archangel and with the trumpet call of God, and the dead in Christ will rise first. After that, we who are still alive and are left will be caught up together with them in the clouds to meet the Lord in the air. And so we will be with the Lord forever. Therefore encourage each other with these words.

And will we recognise our loved ones? J. I. Packer writes: [11]

> *However, as the risen Jesus was recognisable by his disciples, despite the change that resurrection had wrought in him, and as the re-embodied Moses and Elijah were recognisable at the Transfiguration (Matthew 17 v 3-4) and as re-embodied Jewish saints were recognisable at the time of Jesus' rising (Matthew 27 v 52-53), so risen Christians will be recognisable to each other, and joyful reunions beyond this world with believers whom we loved and then lost through death are to be expected.*

What a prospect!

When He comes, our glorious King,
All His ransomed home to bring,
Then anew this song we'll sing:
Hallelujah! What a Saviour! [12]

---

[11] J.I.Packer; *Concise Theology*(p255). IVP
[12] P.P.Bliss; *Man of Sorrows*

Appendix: The Story of Lazarus

John 11

A man named Lazarus was sick. He was from Bethany, the village where Mary and her sister Martha lived. Mary would later pour perfume on the Lord. She would also wipe his feet with her hair. Her brother Lazarus was sick in bed. So the sisters sent a message to Jesus. "Lord," they told him, "the one you love is sick."

When Jesus heard this, he said, "This sickness will not end in death. No, it is for God's glory. God's Son will receive glory because of it."

Jesus loved Martha and her sister and Lazarus. But after he heard Lazarus was sick, he stayed where he was for two more days.

Then he said to his disciples, "Let us go back to Judea."

"But Rabbi," they said, "a short time ago the Jews tried to kill you with stones. Are you still going back there?"

Jesus answered, "Aren't there 12 hours of daylight? A person who walks during the day won't trip and fall. He can see because of this world's light. But when he walks at night, he'll trip and fall. He has no light."

After he said this, Jesus went on speaking to them. "Our friend Lazarus has fallen asleep," he said. "But I am going there to wake him up."

His disciples replied, "Lord, if he's sleeping, he will get better."

Jesus had been speaking about the death of Lazarus. But his disciples thought he meant natural sleep.

So then he told them plainly, "Lazarus is dead. For your benefit, I am glad I was not there. Now you will believe. But let us go to him."

Then Thomas, who was called Didymus, spoke to the rest of the disciples. "Let us go also," he said. "Then we can die with Jesus."

When Jesus arrived, he found out that Lazarus had already been in the tomb for four days. Bethany was less than two miles from Jerusalem. Many Jews had come to Martha and Mary. They had come to comfort them because their brother was dead.

When Martha heard that Jesus was coming, she went out to meet him. But Mary stayed at home.

"Lord," Martha said to Jesus, "I wish you had been here! Then my brother would not have died. But I know that even now God will give you anything you ask for."

Jesus said to her, "Your brother will rise again."

Martha answered, "I know he will rise again. This will happen when people are raised from the dead on the last day."

Jesus said to her, "I am the resurrection and the life. Anyone who believes in me will live, even if he dies. 26 And those who live and believe in me will never die. Do you believe this?"

"Yes, Lord," she told him. "I believe that you are the Christ, the Son of God. I believe that you are the One who was supposed to come into the world."

After she said this, she went back home. She called her sister Mary to one side to talk to her. "The Teacher is here," Martha said. "He is asking for you."

When Mary heard this, she got up quickly and went to him. Jesus had not yet entered the village. He was still at the place where Martha had met him. Some Jews had been comforting Mary in the house. They noticed how quickly she got up and went out. So they followed her. They thought she was going to the tomb to cry there.

Mary reached the place where Jesus was. When she saw him, she fell at his feet. She said, "Lord, I wish you had been here! Then my brother would not have died."

Jesus saw her crying. He saw that the Jews who had come along with her were crying also. His spirit became very sad, and he was troubled.

"Where have you put him?" he asked.

"Come and see, Lord," they replied.

Jesus sobbed.

Then the Jews said, "See how much he loved him!"

But some of them said, "He opened the eyes of the blind man. Couldn't he have kept this man from dying?"

Once more Jesus felt very sad. He came to the tomb. It was a cave with a stone in front of the entrance.

"Take away the stone," he said.

"But, Lord," said Martha, the sister of the dead man, "by this time there is a bad smell. Lazarus has been in the tomb for four days."

Then Jesus said, "Didn't I tell you that if you believed, you would see God's glory?"

So they took away the stone.

Then Jesus looked up. He said, "Father, I thank you for hearing me. I know that you always hear me. But I said this for the benefit of the people standing here. I said it so they will believe that you sent me."

Then Jesus called in a loud voice. He said, "Lazarus, come out!"

The dead man came out. His hands and feet were wrapped with strips of linen. A cloth was around his face.

Jesus said to them, "Take off the clothes he was buried in and let him go."

Many of the Jews who had come to visit Mary saw what Jesus did. So they put their faith in him. But some of them went to the Pharisees. They told the Pharisees what Jesus had done. Then the chief priests and the Pharisees called a meeting of the Sanhedrin.

"What can we do?" they asked. "This man is doing many miraculous signs. If we let him keep on doing this, everyone will believe in him. Then the Romans will come. They will take away our temple and our nation."

One of them spoke up. His name was Caiaphas. He was high priest at that time. He said, "You don't know anything at all! You don't realize what is good for you. It is better if one man dies for the people than if the whole nation is destroyed."

He did not say this on his own. But he was high priest at that time. So he told ahead of time that Jesus would die for the Jewish nation. He also prophesied that Jesus would die for God's children scattered everywhere. He would die to bring them together and make them one.

So from that day on, the Jewish rulers planned to kill Jesus.

Jesus no longer moved around openly among the Jews. Instead, he went away to an area near the desert. He went to a village called Ephraim. There he stayed with his disciples.

It was almost time for the Jewish Passover Feast. Many people went up from the country to Jerusalem. They went there for the special washing that would make them pure before the Passover Feast. They kept looking for Jesus as they stood in the temple area. They asked one another, *"What do you think? Isn't he coming to the Feast at all?"*

But the chief priests and the Pharisees had given orders. They had commanded anyone who found out where Jesus was staying to report it. Then they could arrest him.